The Beguilings

Also by Jessica Raschke and published by Ginninderra Press
Luscious Glass Cage

Jessica Raschke

The Beguilings

With love for Jim Pettigrew.

With gratitude to Melanie Scaife, Allison Colpoys, Bruce Sims, Bridget Stockdale and Michelle Mosiere.

And with thanks to the creature at Dock Inlet who ate *The Beguilings* with gusto.

The Beguilings
ISBN 978 1 74027 609 2
Copyright © text Jessica Raschke 2010
www.jessicaraschke.com
Copyright © cover art and design Allison Colpoys 2010

First published 2010
Reprinted 2016

Ginninderra Press
PO Box 3461 Port Adelaide SA 5015
www.ginninderrapress.com.au

Contents

bleeding celebration	7
the howlings	8
continuous	11
awakening fury	12
Sin Section I	13
Sin Section II	15
the heroine's memory	16
love thievery	17
the lover lost	18
reassurances	19
explanation failure	20
doctrine breath	21
truth flesh	23
time it took	24
the molten moment	25
mercury mountains	26
the straddle sorts	28
hemmed-in secret	30
predictable cosmos woman	31
breaking curvy corners	33
stomping perfections	34
red frays	35
captured element	37
grievous constellation	38
salvages	39
simple wild	40
wicked confession	41
impulse I	42
impulse II	43
the beguilings	44

bleeding celebration

a celebration of agitation
my lips smooth enigma curls
an agitation of celebration
my bleeds creep into these words

the howlings

amid the shadows are whispers true
ensouled with wordings,
concerning me:

every single collapse is divine
but the howling, it is mine

there is no quiet, never more
and what is spirit, is quiet stored
an internal hum, it burns insight
from silent beats, devices tight

my brittle tongue, it licks the air
breaks into stars, then beaming sheets
they spiral around and meet my feet
grip my body to earthen deeps

here I am, fortified,
and here I ache, petrified,
a star shine cripple,
still whispering:

every single collapse is divine
but the howling, it is mine

questing/
my body's transparency
desisting/
my soul's serenity

they turned to molten mirror tears,
and from their interiors my reflection goes:

what can be more myself than I?
when others are also somewhat myself?
are they all, then, more than me?

(why is myself so far from me?)

tell me:
what silver-crowned creator imagined this?

a bleeding battle, it threw me here:
and I was christened a void full of innocence
and I waited for experience to encounter me
then I pummelled the lands frayed from bloodiness
then I carved through my heart flat from wistfulness
and I set my time ablaze with broodiness
and I am shattered from disgrace with my overflows

my life's advances, when it passes, will shrink
into stunned island shards, lying stark

my emptiness lies in those indifference swamps
and it fills the plush heavens, to vacuums

but, the void was where I started
the void is warm, like home

why blister our deaths with overload,
why banish collated wisdoms away from here,
why bury them deep in eternal realms,
those cloistered quarters, infinities

yes, the void was where I started
the void is warm, like home

can a beginning only live
where an ending ceased to be

there are no walls, releasing me
there are only walls, creating me

it whispers true, my silent soul

every single collapse is divine
but the howling, it is mine

continuous

love,
like life,
is one
long
continuous
breath.

until one,
or the other,
or both…

awakening fury

why does death awaken
as I am coming of age

it's a cautionary tale

I'm furious and I'm full
from being fed uneasiness

so…
let it happen
so…
just allow me to be

a cautionary tale

I am without a name *and*
this is something *yes*
this is something

I am without a name *but*
I am one thing *yes*
I am one thing

remember
just allow me to be

remember
let it happen

I am one thing *and*
this is something *yes*
this is something

remember
worth mentioning

Sin Section I

slice a section, sexing skin
yes
tear it from my love
cut a bit so tiny
a potent happening thing

your language does not save me
your words are just skewed sense

slice a section, sexing skin
again
with those brutal moral arms
take this button
steeped in history

and

slice a section, sexing skin
yes
designed to measure
your limits

really – it's just a compass
really – it's just a map

for pleasuring
now torn

without love
all gone

without sin
now mourned

spread my love skin, see it open
probe it, arms of pain
bully my insides, for a viewing
tweak around, smothered cries

yes
the gods are filled, failure
equipped to falter, heavy wings
their shame, protected
slice a section, sexing skin

Sin Section II

please don't make it gape
don't open it any more
this is my lustrous section
okay
a beckoning place named sin

stripping by your eyes
doused in cruel intent
the expansion
without your heart
a strident slap
against my nature

remember…

the gaping was
for you
it opened
for you

but the pretext
was just a front
ready-made
for your
destroys

the heroine's memory

loss leeches my memory
loss empties my blood of its burn
my head rightly placed for scorching
gas flaming, fastening my breath
to its ends

...this attempt, it is an effort...
...so I'm assuming there will be...

reverence for this act
and
celebration of my death

a heroine is a blazing human
a heroine is me, sapped of air
a heroine is me, assuming
a heroine is me

you will know it when you see me:

...yes...

the one who failed to live

love thievery

my grave is not my life
my love not in your mourning
so, smear your smirking tears
glimmers of treasures in their sights

please
can you see:
there is theft
in your hunger

you rob
you call it treasure
you rob
you call it for salvation
you rob
you say from heartache
you rob
you say from love

but please
can you see:
there is theft
in your hunger

the lover lost

your spinning heights won't earth those feet
from the crumble, when she goes
your peppy laughs won't pump her heart
for more life, when she goes

she was a lover
destined for this

(erasure)

a lover
fated for you

she was a lover
brimming with synergies
of the exclusive and of the true

she was a lover

and tomorrow
she ceases
and tomorrow
from you

reassurances

mysteries are our reassurances
we keep failing from ignorance

remind ourselves
we have been wise

all we have
are the absences

explanation failure

no explanation
no failure
a mere lapsing into memories

(borrowed)

a savage skinscape
bloodied by desires

(buried)

failures, choke
explanations, liberate

skinscapes
the steps to horizons

unheard
unsavaged
unborn

skinscapes
transformed
into mines

doctrine breath

why write down a doctrine
why not love it in a breath

really
there is no posterity
in the motionless

really
there is no matter
in the inks you place them in

really

the ones that sound the same:

they are muddied
and
they are stuck
and
they are wailing
for some meaning

they are struggling
for some movement
and for something, somewhere to

explain
explain
explain

elusive language batters
casts adrift the sentiments

really
live your meaning in your breath

really
fill your airs with your contained

yes
you sense their gentle presence
yes
you sense the honests within

truth flesh

to start with

a newborn calls it true
but can truth be born like flesh
can its lungs ache for refresh
can its lungs ache for more renew

shady hopes for the eternal
drawn from shallows maternal

a fellowship of ancestry
embedded in matters made born
infects degradation in the flourishing
damages impassive beginning forms

purity is like illusion
an imagined fortune spent
purity is the loss of life
what the flesh has

to start with

time it took

the time it took to see it
the time it took to see me

time, it was taken,
but still, it stood waiting
time, it was taken,
and still, it tried to see me

the trees have spread in rings
their energies have dwindled in their sighs
they lie, in generous sprawling,
in seductive clumsy rows

the past now sits bracing
the past expects it's facing
what once were futures
what now flies aloft

the time,
it took

the molten moment

the quality of the bones
cannot shake
the tremors in
the bloodied iron will
cannot thwart
this fated caving in

a broken silvering beast
a whitening artery form
now
a home for dusty hoping
now
a home for foolish whims

these bones are sutured whites
fractured by their moves

hush

this waiting must be broken
so bring me
the molten moment

hush

so bring me
the one
moment

hush

the one
to be
my end

mercury mountains

from his itching memory
simmers countless sunken dreams
a moment ago he was a hero
now he's grating bones and skins

now, he wears a sullied halo
once, it was white
once, it cast an aura

this is…his story

the splinters of experience
pierce all his form

this is…an ode

to his death
to his sleeping start
to his life

he once held fire in his hands
he once built mountains from mercury
a fellow dreamer plunged him there
among the collapsed ethers in

he wishes to have it all
to have it all again

he remembers the happy fouls
and the pleasing plunderings

from here…
it was worthwhile…

all those
leisured wonders
all those
younger whims

the straddle sorts

straddle me, pretend bravely
built of overblown and lashing fires
contain your fury at my innards
clench the denying of your roar

your clawing is deceitful
it claims its kindness shines
yet its honesty sits
in its blinding twinkle sharps
its lying truth strikes
as clean as vicious force

your bravado
is not heroic
for no mythology
accompanies
your mane

your ideas remain unpunished
they are rewarded by the gods
your ideas hold hollow promise
they are honoured by your sorts

so…
straddle me with a promise
to build a better place
straddle me with noises
to build a new domain

(yes)

a new home

one

for those

like you:

(they are)

the feckless/
the sinless/
the sexless/

they are

the overblown sorts

hemmed-in secret

it's no secret
some things await
away from a hemmed-in dress

directed by distant rulerships
the outfitting generates misfits
a sure thing, a harassed future
they are burdened by bottled ins

some things await
away from a hemmed-in dress

predictable cosmos woman

predict
the naked woman
the arch symbol

our everything…

our cosmos
our universe

yes

our everything…

including
(you guessed it)
all those saucy things:

desirability
vulnerability
fuckability
virginity
penetrability
frigidity

yes…

predict
the naked woman

motif
the naked woman

relief
the naked woman

predict
the naked woman

breaking curvy corners

corners are built for hidings
and your container flesh

…

well

…

it seems

…

well

…

it's just
inconvenient

better to bustle and to button
all that sits among the breasts
cornerless features that they are
not hidings but answers blessed
this is feminine construction
with awareness on every mole
this is feminine construction
short of hidings among the curves

stomping perfections

inside their perfections
growl fretful little jeers
a social eclipse, not a sunrise
as cloaks of victory fall on feet

you ask:

what of their perfections

they are boulders at their soles
striking grounds of foiled tightness

there's no land of great release

envy circles their perfections
their virtues are carved by shackle sharps
their bones are dreaming of their coveting
and then – after simmering – they come busy:

shattering into fatal
and near (im)perfect
ends

red frays

she slides into the red robes
with oiled hands she holds her prizes
the residues of all the lovers gone
and she watches them quietly
as her breath ousts

> *sprawling*
> *deflating*
> *plumes*

(…the ones
that carried her
and her hope…)

this hope
catches form
this hope
brittles away
this hope
just held in
by frayed fabrics

…and now…

her eyes are veiled with aloof
her trembles are handed over:
to him

he's a prize
he regrets being
he's a brutalised hero
he fought to be

and now…
they stand on the flimsy together

and now…
they walk on the fragile together

the red robes soiled with pretence
the oiled hands shattered from fraughts
the hope is still expecting
and the hope it floats in waiting
it knows that they will come:
more prizes in her hands

captured element

snap that thunder
with one more hand
display it in your palm
display it
that one
only one
(yet captured)
element

grievous constellation

look aside
at the grievous constellation
at the whirling fade-out

look aside
at the shady hallowed darkness
at the unfurling procession of deep

look inside
you're performing
a glorious descent

look inside
you're remaining
another glittering haze

look inside
defer just a fraction
look inside
and be gone
look inside
once again
look inside
start to grieve
look inside
it's all over

your self
it has faded
your constellation
it has gone

salvages

salvage the male menace
redeem the female plague
divisions decorate our thinking
inflaming justice with fireballs

the menace and the plague
pert forces dropping pain
the menace and the plague
sparkling laughter, entertained

our heads ache
delightfully
our heavens crumble
brightly
we are familiar
with this drowning
the sodden wetness
among our thinkings

and so love
hates our deviates
and so love
finger stretches
and so love
sedates us
and so love
evades us

simple wild

*you found that simple truth
when you hated me like wild*

oh!
my little psychopompous pet
cast a leash around my neck

oh!
this journeying is natural
it's not brave nor risqué

*you found that simple truth
when you hated me like wild*

wicked confession

(yes)

confess your lust
declare your pain
your liberty is
to return evil

'one dreams of revenge'

(oh yes)

confess your lust
declare your pain
to return evil
is your liberty

'one dreams of revenge'

(oh)

impulse I

brutal force on your arms
shallow impulse in your heart
forget it's just good fucking
recall the delicate ground you're in

impulse II

slide into the impulse
glide along its terrain
enjoy its formless rumbling tones
channelling those angel-devil grips

to the impulse:

its reverberations are not sound
yet it hosts the proudest truths

it pulses for my in:
for my elsewhere
that is my *smashing*
for my elsewhere
that is my *splitting*
for my elsewhere
that is *my soul*

the beguilings

by the way
perhaps I'm tricking

by the way
a smiling type

by the way
perhaps we're fretting

by the way
the beguilings strike

www.ingramcontent.com/pod-product-compliance
Lightning Source LLC
Chambersburg PA
CBHW062206100526
44589CB00014B/1981